Polychotomy

Adelia Jupiter

Mrs. Ross,
Thank you for turning "writer" from dream to goal.

Riley,
Thank you for being the patron saint of this book.

My Jupiters,
Thank you for muddling through with me.

Murphy Newt,
Thank you for showing me what true love feels like.

All my exes,
Thanks for the inspiration.

Contents

Contents

Rebirth

Sandcastles

I am building sandcastles
from the wet sand on the shore.
My brothers didn't like my designs,
they only had me scraping moats.
So, I venture out on my own.
Quietly.
My father helps my brothers
build spires and doors and walls.
Did my mother watch me go?

I build what I can as fast as I can
before the next wave comes.
I shove together
what my little hands can gather.
I want my castle to be better,
grander,
more intricate,
but I only have these two little hands
and the next wave is coming
and I don't know how to
build spires or doors or walls.
So, I scrape
and I scrape,
and they laugh as the wave
tries to take their castle,
and I try to block the water
but I only have these two little hands
and the mound that could've been
my castle washes away.

They continue
to line their castle with shells
as I try to mimic their wall
to protect my formless fortress.
The next wave comes.
My wall goes.

What was I even protecting?

Screaming

I'm in my crib,
my brother is in his,
and I'm screaming
and waiting for
someone—
anyone—
to hold me,
to soothe me.
The world is big
and scary
and everything is new
including me.

I'm a child
storming off to my room
slamming doors,
laying on the floor,
kicking
and screaming,
waiting for
someone—
anyone—
to tell me
that it makes sense
why I hurt so much,
that they know why:
they know how to fix me.

I'm an adult
and I still don't know
how to get someone—
anyone—
to notice me
if I'm not screaming.
My insides are so messed up
from the years of
reverberation,
I don't know
if I'm screaming at
you or me.
I just know
I'm so alone
with my whispers.

Work

On his deathbed
my grandfather
was asked for one last
parting wisdom
for me and my brothers.
He chose the word,
"Work."
I grew up hearing
the trickle down
advice from my father,
"If you're going to be
a ditch digger,
be the best
ditch digger
you can be."
I grew up
with a father choosing
work
instead of family
because that's what it meant
to provide.
So, as I entered the
work-
force, I was overwhelmed
by the future
I didn't want.
In my fear of being
hogtied for capitalist pigs,
I've given up freedoms.

But in this cage I have built
inside a cage I can't escape,
I have still found
work.

My work
is learning how to love
in ways that were never modeled
and how to be a person
with this cobbled brain.

My work
is crafting something
terrible and beautiful
and reflective
with one hand
and with the other,
simply holding another's hand.
It is also knowing
when to drop everything,
to hold my own pain back
from complete destruction.

My work
is taking up space
while taking up as few
resources as possible
without the stitches in my
mind ripping.

My work
is hard and thankless.
I am still
at work
every waking hour,
just as my father is.

My work
is "love"
until I die.

And I have been
broke
ever since.

Moving boxes

I feel around
at the edges of where
belonging
used to be.
It's an empty box
that can't be
filled with stuff,
can't be
taped closed,
can't be
shipped off.

It resembles the rooms
of all the places
I once called
home.

The only way
I know how
to fill it
is with people.
But the edges,
they itch
and cut at my organs,
and I try to pack
the box full enough
that the sides bow
and stretch
and resemble

something organic.

But there is no
squish to it;
it can only
rupture.
I can only
hemorrhage
people
because I don't know how
to sit in this room

alone.

Blanket

I don't care
how many times
I have to do it,
I will rip apart
this thick hide
I grew to keep me
warm in the void
to sew together
something gentler.

Let me weave together
the threads of my fate
until I've made it into
a blankie the child
in me can use as a cloak
as they direct the dance
of the autumn leaves
with their twig wand.

I'll wrap the blanket around me
and any of my people
who need shelter from
the catastrophes
we couldn't avoid.
Let it shield us
from the sky that's
burning away—
if only it wasn't metaphorical.

I will crack open
with lightning
to join forces
with the constellations
to tell stories
that guide us home
and away from the fathers
who wouldn't —
couldn't—
didn't
protect us.

I will come
undone
and undone
and undone
until I'm something
worth keeping together
to keep us together.

These scars are the
seams where I've
mended myself
after hurting myself
because I couldn't stand
being myself.

I am Frankenstein
and his monster

and I am afraid
of myself
and I am afraid
of the light
but I will keep
going
because maybe
I'll learn to love
who I've created
under this blanket.

Arrhythmic

It's louder at night
in the quiet
where I have nowhere to go
except for the room I grew up in—
the door still barricaded with judgment.
And in this room
where there is only the sound
of the fan,
screams deafen me.
Every hot tear
from every year
since I was three
patter

      patter
  patters
like an arrhythmic metronome.
I am expected to feel
safe in this room
because outside there is a reality
I can't face.
But in here, I still play make-believe
with the monsters in my head
because they paid more attention
to me than anyone ever did.
They hug me
and tell me I'm better off dead.
And nowhere is safe
but in your arms

but they are folding
around someone else
in your grown-up bed
in the house that's all yours
that I used to call mine.
And I need to find a way
to be okay with it
because if I can't
there will be
no safe places left.

Home

When I finally have a home,
it will be full of love
and dog hair
and the smell of cinnamon.

When I finally have a home,
the walls will be painted
as dark as I'd like.
I'll have plush carpet and
washable rugs.
The cabinet knobs will
be in the shape of bugs and hands
and there will be a million
tiny details (secrets)
for people to discover.

In the center of the living room
will be a table big enough
for me to do puzzles
with 2,000–hell, 5,000 pieces
in front of whatever show
that I want to watch
and no one will complain
that it's been there for months
because I will live alone.

The dining room
will have a big table too
for me to seat all of my friends

and partners
for a different kind of puzzle.
If they need to stay the night,
I won't need to ask
for permission
because I will live alone.

And there in the office,
that will be my studio.
It will be as messy as art is.
And no one will touch my materials
thinking that they're trash
because I will live alone.

When I finally have an actual home,
I won't have to compromise
my accessibility
for someone else's aesthetics
because I will live alone.

My bedroom will be viridian green
with fake plants everywhere
because they won't die
when the depression comes
because it will come
and I won't have to
explain myself to anyone.
It won't be crammed full of
the stuff I've collected

over four lives
because my things
won't be deemed unimportant
and unworthy of a proper place.
My things will finally
have a home.

And no one will touch my stuff
without asking.

In the kitchen,
the sink will be full
of dishes instead
of resentment.
The trash will be taken out
before the bugs come
(believe it or not).
Things will get done
when they need to,
not when other people
think they should.
But it'll be cleaner
than everyone would expect
from me
because finally I'll feel
a sense of ownership.

And no one will touch my stuff
without asking.

I can have every closet to myself.
No one will tell me
I have too much stuff
because finally I won't
have to try to fit where
there is no room for me.

And no one will touch my stuff
without asking.

I'll have a doggie door
for when the fatigue
chains me to the bed.
I'll have autofeeders
so I don't forget to
feed the real
love of my life.
I can train him
to speak with buttons
using my voice
to tell me
he loves me
and I'll have no reason
to feel embarrassed
because no one will
be around to laugh at me.

And when my partners
spend the night,

I'll have to get *them*
toothbrushes,
they can borrow my
oversized hoodies.

But everyone will eventually
leave
and I will be able to
have my quiet
and do my puzzles.

When I finally have a home,
I will finally be able to breathe.

Please be quiet

Please be quiet.
I don't want to think those thoughts.
I don't want to stare down my reality
that is rooted in rot.

I want my roots to nourish.
I want to be covered in moss,
swallowed whole by Mother Earth,
dying

Nope! Not those thoughts!

I want to be flying
instead of diving,
kasplat

Nope!

Take it from another angle,
sharp, jagged angles

No! Stop!

Please! I want to live!

I don't want to know
that the only way out is down.

Everyone is staring at me

with shovels in their hands
saying,
"I wish there was more I could do."

If you can't help me out,
could you please stop
shoveling dirt into my mouth?

I can't breathe

I can't breathe
I can't breathe
I can't I can't I can't

I want to live.

Mor(t)ality

Again and again and again

To be known
is to be loved,
so you must know me
in my entirety
immediately.
You must know my every
thought
or else you will
misunderstand me
and if you misunderstand me
then you won't love me
and if you don't love me
then I am
wrong.

I feel you slipping away,
I must be a bad person.
I must've done something wrong.
Tell me what I've done wrong.

You tell me to stop doing
this.
This constant *aaaaahhhh!*
I can't.
If I stop then
you will misunderstand me
and if you misunderstand me
then you won't love me
and if you don't love me

then I am wrong.

So I talk
and talk
and talk.

Shut up!
You are making things worse!

I have to be honest.
I have to be honest or else
I am morally wrong.
But I have lied.
I have lied
and lied
and lied
to protect myself.

Little girls get
punished
if they're not
perfect.
Little girls punish
themselves
if they have to
protect themselves.

I can't be known
if I'm not honest.

Honesty is love.

I am making myself
unlovable.

Let me
explain
explain
explain
everything.

Little girl
thinks having
no walls
can save her.

See me
see me
see me.

You do not.
You do not want
to step into a burning city.
You ride away
on your white horse.

But this wouldn't be happening
if you understood.

I text
and text
and text.

Shut! Up!
You are making things worse!
Put the phone down!
This will not make them
come back!

I don't know how to stop
I don't know how to stop
I don't know how to stop

Put the phone down
Put the phone down
Put the phone down!

"Please come back.
I know I can try harder.
I know you can love me
again.
I don't care
if it hurts me.
I know we can work through it."

God, shut up!
They don't want to work through it!
You are crazy!

Stop.
Stopstopstopstopstop

I am lovable.
If I can learn to love me
then so can someone else.

I text him
I text him
I text him

"I am healed!
See how I am healed?
I am having clear thoughts!"

Why are you still texting him?

I don't know how to stop.
I don't know what's wrong with me.

It's the MDD
or the GAD
or the ADHD
or the BPD.

You have no impulse control.

But these are compulsions.

Do I have OCD too?

Google
Google
Google

No, no, not OCD.
One of the others.

Are we sure?

Google
Google
Google

To be known is to be loved.
If I don't know myself,
I can't love myself.
If I don't know myself,
I will never be able to
explain myself.
If I can't explain myself
I will never be understood.
If I'm never understood,
no one will ever love me.
If no one will ever love me
then I will always be bad

inside and out.

He no longer responds.

He is right to do so.

I text
and text
and text.

Little girl
is ready for
a nap.

Maybe in a year
I will stop.
Maybe in a year
someone new
will try to know me.
Maybe in a year
I will finally
be good.

I can't possibly be
the only person who feels
pressure building in between
skin and muscle and soul,
bubbling and distorting,
but when the pressure
crushes my bones,
I feel uncontrollably alone.
The loss of control
is hyperinflating
my lungs and dread.

You make me desperate
for puncture wounds
to release the pressure,
for popping air pockets
so that I can breathe.
You make me desperate
to be in your arms,
but you will never
understand:
I have no
control over me.

These words escape
from my mouth in
an attempt to
exhale,
but I cannot breathe

your words in
when you have no words
to say.
So, as these words
stumble from my mouth,
and tears stutter down my cheeks,
your teeth chatter
against empty smiles of
uncertainty.
You make me desperate
for stability.

This desperation
is strangulation.
Asphyxiating from your snores
while I lie awake in your room
where your fan clicks with no rhythm.
You sleep with the deep breaths
that I can no longer produce
after hiking alone to your place
with your car parked out front
in the middle of the night
in a heat I can't take
in a terror I can't shake.

You roll over away from me,
your back facing me
and I wrap my arms around you,
my cheek resting in the divet

of your shoulder blade.
I feel your heart beat
the back of your ribcage
and I don't care that
you don't care
because your heartbeat
reminds me I'm still breathing,
I still have reasons
for breathing.

But those reasons don't matter
because I still can't get enough oxygen
when I'm away from you.
My brain thinks it's dying
and tries to make my body follow.
I hyperventilate and scream
and when I reach out to you
over tiny letters on a screen
you turn off your phone
and leave me alone.
You abandon me.
When I fight my way out
with jagged scars that don't heal,
I ask you what happened
and you say it was just too much,
you didn't want to deal with it,
you didn't know how.

Your "I don't know" became

"I don't care" and you didn't
even realize.
So, now on your list
I've become the crazy one.
I didn't drink
or smoke
or lie away my problems,
but I trusted you enough
to show you them with their
masks off.
And I was so desperate for you
to see what I saw,
but now I'm just desperate
for the air that you stole
when I said goodbye
and I walked away
from all those things
that you didn't say.

Gunk

He tells me,
he's not in the mood
for sex tonight.
A reasonable request but
my reasoning
leaves my body.

I am dunked
into military-grade
Gunk.
Gunk named
"What good are you
if he doesn't even want
to fuck you?"
Named
"You remind him
of his ex."
Named
"He loves sex,
so how disgusting
must you be."
Named
"You will die
alone."
And I walk away.

I go take a shower.
I scrub
and scrub

and scrub,
but the gunk
doesn't come off,
it just seeps into me
further.
Though my skin
looks polished and
gunkless,
it is in my organs.
it has become bronchial.
And I'm left coughing up
as I towel off,
"I'm okay! Really!"
which is aerosol gunk
named
"Why don't you love me?"
As I dress myself,
I cough up,
"I'm just tired,"
which is the brand name of,
"This is the only thing
I know how to give."
And my eyes turn black
and they sign
"I am worthless
without this,"
but he's already
avoiding my gaze.
Until it reaches my heart

and the beats sound like
"Fuck me.
Fuck me.
Fuck me."
But when was the last time
he laid his head
on my chest?

My blood
is boiled sludge,
and I do not know
how to survive this
tar
without getting paved over,
but I would let him
walk all over me
if it meant that I
could be flayed
and cleansed,
so that when I tell him
that I love him
it isn't sticky.

And I'm jealous
of all the bodies
those hands have touched
including his
because they're not mine.
And I'm jealous

of those hands.
And it hurts
in ways that this poem
cannot express.
And it is isolation,
and I am the jailer,
and I still do not know
how to break myself out
because this gunk is thick
and my eyes are black
and my heart
doesn't
beat
right.

Yes (No)

How could you know?
When my mouth says yes,
how could you guess
that inside I'm screaming
"No."
My body moves the way it
should,
rehearsals guiding
my muscle memory.
The only thing missing
is a particular kind of
wetness
but even that eventually
comes
so that my body
isn't torn apart.
You finish inside
and I'm left dripping
with your
wetness.
You ask how it was,
and I say "Great,
I'm just gonna clean up."
I go to the bathroom
and sob
and try not to vomit at the
stickiness
between my thighs.
I put my face back

together
and calm my swollen eyes
and try not to think
about my swollen lips
but I'm sore
and it's nagging,
"This is how they love you."
I open the door
and pad over to them
naked
and curl our bodies
together
as they bask in the
afterglow
that irradiates me.

Thank you for not doing the laundry

Thank you
for not doing the laundry.

I look at the pile of clothes
with a heart full of love.
This is the product
of you trying to
keep yourself alive.

These clothes
do not belong in your casket.
If this is how they
keep you breathing,
they belong on the floor.

I see the way
the light scatters over
the different colors,
different textures
and to me, it looks like art.

It's okay if you're never ready
to take down the installation.
It's not a sign of your failure.

This is your gallery showing
and your work is meaningful.
I have come here to see you,
and your work moves me.

Look at these beautiful
signs of life;
I am grateful to witness it.

And it's okay too
if you're ready for a new exhibit,
but you need to call in your crew
to help with the take down
and set up.
That's what a crew is for.
Just tell us what your vision is.

Don't close the gallery.
Keep making more art.

Thank you
for not doing the laundry.

I've moved on, I promise

I was sick for months,
my body failing me,
my mind unable to help,
and that's
when you left me.
The words weren't spoken,
but you were no longer
there.
I wasn't pulling my weight
when I was trying
to keep my weight
from drowning me.
The weight of my reality
pulled you into stoic
resentment.
And I will
Never
forgive that.

You said I needed too much
when I stopped asking
for anything.
I couldn't
clean out the fridge.

Who cares about the fridge?
I was too busy coughing
until I couldn't breathe,
and begging my body to move,

and trying to get my brain to not
murder the person
you said you loved.
Why didn't you love me
when you said you would?

I never lied to you
about who I was.
I never hid from you.
I didn't know I had to.
But when you realized
that you couldn't fix me,
you fell out of love with me.
Did you ever really love me?
In this story,
you are the bad guy
and I am the consequence.
And I will
Never
forgive you.

Good Grief

Okay.
One.
Two.
Three.
I take a breath
and accept how
this hole in my chest
was formed.
I breathe into the pain
as fingernails
drag across sinew
and catch on tendons
and remind myself
that the pain is real
but the injury, mental.
That, though my mind
is filled with the memory
of nightmares,
my body is safe,
and I remind myself
that it's good
for my body to be safe
and not following you
into the places where the living
can't go.
It's good that I can't follow yet.
I don't understand how it
could ever be good
to not be where you are,

but they tell me it's good
and I don't trust myself
when I've lost my mind.
I don't know how I'll ever
get my mind back
when it was buried with you,
how this hole will ever be filled
because it's in the shape of you
it echoes of the things
I wish I had said.
My eyelids burn with afterimages
of all the things
I shouldn't have done.
I'm sweating from this hell, but
my bones are frozen
without your warmth
and no one else can
seep into my skin.
My love,
I miss you,
I'm safe,
please come get me soon.

I want to shove my hands
through the skin of my chest,
break open my rib cage,
and crush my heart
like a soda bottle.

I want to rip it out
and throw it in the
recycler,
so that something else
can use it
for something more
productive
than hurting.
And this isn't enough.

I need to rummage around
for my esophagus
until I can break it off
and hook my lungs up
directly to a machine.

Put me on life support,
make me into a robot,
tear apart the fibers of my muscles
string them together
dry and beat them
like linen
put on a loom

so you can still
sleep with me at night
I still feel too crowded
there's no room
left
I have to scoop out
all my internal organs
just to have the space
enough to feel
but that's not enough
open up my flesh
lay it out
crush my bones
release the demons
it's not enough
I'm dead
and it's still
too much

Possession

It's finally crashing into me:
all the years of men
using and discarding my body,
who care only about sowing
but never weaving.
They would say anything
to try to fill their lonely pit
with the hole inside me,
but these two negative spaces
cannot make a positive.

I have never had
a healthy relationship
with sex.
Before I even really understood
how it worked—
sex education in 2009 Ohio
being what it was—
I had boys whispering the word
"sex"
in my ear:
They loved watching me wince.
The very first time
my body was part
of the act,
I was inside my head
screaming "no,"
but the voice out of my mouth
said "yes."

This was a punishment,
the other voice occupying my mind
said so.
She said it was what I deserved.
She grabbed hold of my body,
made it do all the things
a good girl should do
when getting fucked
while she forced me to watch.

I have an ex who thought
I was possessed.

I have always felt
like a possession,
but I've never been very good
at sitting on the shelf.
Once they put me up there,
and the fear of gathering dust sets in,
I will fling myself off at their feet—
no matter how far the fall.
They'd wonder why I'm all broken,
and I'd wonder why
they don't love me anymore.
I wonder if they ever really did.
I know my actions
don't match my words
don't match my thoughts
don't match my self

that's split even further.
People get turned around
in my polychotomy
and that disturbs them.
It disturbs me,
but I can't escape myself,
so I have to learn how to not
throw parts of myself away
so they can fill it with whatever
they think will make them stay.
Being whole is more important
than being seen as good
by men who my existence disturbs.

Rather, I'm a bitter god whose
two brothers drew the better sticks.
Life has banished me from the mountain
but this is my domain now
and these mortal men are
not nearly enough
to throw me off
my throne.

So, when I touch myself,
it is still out of defiance
and it is still laced with disgust,
but one day I'll learn
that it's okay that I need
love to be there too.
And one day it will be.

The winds that leave/The roots that stay

You were caught
in the winds that left you.
Carried and settled,
carried and settled,
carried,
your roots have
never been given the chance
to grow.

I stood here
howling back at the wind
branches wild in the sky,
and I caught you.
You passed through
branch and twig and
on your way down,
I hoped you find the soil
instead of the breeze.

There you can lean
against my trunk
and hold onto my bark
as you finally let
your roots
dig deep into the earth
and find mine there,
find the whole forest's.
With your roots intact,
you can learn to grow

beside me
instead of
against me.

But if your roots
ever come loose,
I will hold onto them,
I will stand for us both.
And in this forest,
if the wind finds you
and carries you away,
I know that you will soon
be caught once more
here in the forest.
You will have the chance
to try again
and my roots that
nourish the forest
will still nourish you.

I deserve a sweater

You can't say I didn't try.
I tried so hard that I forgot
to enjoy this mortal life.
Which may mean
I wasn't trying enough,
but it probably means
I was trying too much.
I just want to feel like someone
sees me, feels for me, romanticizes me
the way I do for them.
This tired indifference,
this repetitive epiphany
that I am collateral
to be swept away
is making me bitter.
These people who only have room for me
when it's convenient,
who don't acknowledge the efforts I make.
I don't need constant praise,
just maybe a gold star
every once in a while.

Maybe.

Or maybe I deserve a real star
and the universe around it.
Maybe I deserve everything.
Maybe I want someone's
oceans and storms

and dust and burrows.
I want someone's everything
some of the time.

I want to shiver from
exposure and low-lit whispers.
I want them to commit me to muscle memory
like my brilliance might blind them.
I want them to hold onto the memories
I'm doomed to forget.
I want my fluid reality
to feel steady around them.

What if I could scrape off
all of these layers of beige
painted with kisses and promises
so that I could see what vibrant color
burns where I'm forgotten?
What if I could pull out the cloth
from inside my chest
where all of my tears get soaked up?
What if I could dye it
with that burning hue?
If I could fashion it into a sweater,
Would you wear it?
Or would it be left in the back of your closet
or under your bed with your ex's things
that you can't get rid of?
If I could wear it myself...
Would I even care if you wanted it?

Let them think
what they want.
Let them say
what they want.

The mirror
that mouths,
"Fair enough,"
can never reflect
the vision of me
that I see in my head.
I can never
stand before it
post-op
because there are no
ops to be had.

The most damage
I've taken has been from
running away
from seeming crazy.
I feel the hum
of the universe
threatening to
burst me apart.
It brings me to my knees,
grasping at the mulch
in my childhood playground.
My eyes glaze over

with cinema blue
as I watch myself
in this broken mirror scene
try to come back into
my body with razors on my flesh
or fingers down my throat.

Their thought reduction
doesn't feed me.

Every week
I have therapy in
the neighborhood
where I was promised
forever and
now have *never again.*
I keep myself warm
with the bridges
I've had to burn
just to remind myself
not to go jumping
into the river below.
This is as close
to the sound of silence as
I can keep.

They cannot haunt me
any better
than my own choices.

I got kicked out of my home
by a different forever
because I wasn't silent about
who I was when people
went looking for answers.
I had to go back to people
who never asked
if I was okay
after they checked the news—
they were more interested
in yelling at me
for this silence
that everyone seems
so desperate for me to have,
though they are who
taught me how to scream.
But my inability
to shut the fuck up
has lead to people
who had silence
thrust upon them
finding comfort
in their community that
shouldn't exist—
isn't allowed to grieve.
Silence is only a gift
if it is chosen.
It is a gift
I gave back.

They can think
what they want.
They can say
what they want.

I've been blamed
for murder
because I dared
break up with a boy.
Murder!
And I took that weight
because the person that they
should've been blaming
got put down
with 30 rounds.
They needed to point fingers
somewhere
and his parents
already had their fingers
grasping at two unmarked graves.
He told me he was sober...
The autopsy said
he changed his mind.
It's the only thing
that's made me question
if I protected myself
wrong.
So, I ate that hate
and grieved alone

because my grief
is small and unimportant and
I have no idea where to bury it.

They can have that
silence for themselves,
but they don't want
their own advice.

I lose my mind
and lose my way
and lose my life
and I still come back
to love myself more
because I am the only
voice that matters
and I say
"keep going.

Consummation

This is the wedding dress
that's never met an aisle.
Folded over and shoved away,
clinging to my closet like a curse,
it's the uniform
of my skeletons.
They stand at attention,
waiting for a dead future—
the bride I'll never be
decomposing beneath their feet:
murdered,
skinned,
and eaten.
Resources deconstructed from the bone
are the only things I carried with me into
everything that was coming.
This autocannibalism is
the most necessary thing I've ever done.
It's what lets me step into my closet
so I can shake the dirt off this dress
and say, "I survived."

Ascension

Thalassic

You have learned how to
sail in your lakes,
perhaps even when they're angry.
You put your ship away,
when its surface grows solid, and
you learned to survive
off its bounty
through carving circles
like rituals.

But you come to my ocean
and you are scared of the waves,
of the hurricanes,
of the depths.
And you blame the ocean
for being an ocean
though it was here
before your gods
that let you crawl
out of it.

You come without tribute
claiming to know
all the ways of water,
yet you do not even know
a single shanty.

You meet me at low tide
unable to imagine my waves
towering over
the mightiest ships.
You are hubris
in a dingy.

The only way to
save yourself
is to leave the ocean behind,
leave its unending beauty
and its power

or

to humble yourself,
admit that you know
only of lakes
and allow yourself
to learn
how to navigate
with no shore in sight.

Two weeks ago

Why is it so weird and uncomfortable
for me to tell someone I just met
that I almost killed myself
two weeks ago?
Why is it not met with the same
interest as if I were to announce
I got married two weeks ago
or I had a baby two weeks ago?
Why is that made to seem
like a me problem
and not a them problem
or a society problem
for not raising them
to meet sadness with
the same care and curiosity as joy.

I am alive!
I wanted to die,
But I'm alive!
How curious!
How wonderful!
How wondrous!
Why is it a conversation stopper
instead of starter?

Why should I be made to feel
like my greatest triumph
should not be openly,
explosively celebrated?

Why am I met with sad eyes?
I survived! I'm here telling you!

Don't be afraid to explore
the depths that we are all capable of.
Don't let the fear of
saying the wrong thing
get in the way of
saying the right thing.

I almost killed myself
two weeks ago
and I won't let that
be shuffled away.

I almost killed myself
two weeks ago.
I told my parents
if I didn't get medical intervention
that actually worked
then I'd be dead within the year.
This week is my last of three
where I have had the privilege
of tripping on a dissociative psychedelic
that my parents were desperate enough
to pay for because in America,
insurance impedes life-saving treatment.
I can feel all my feelings
safely for the first time

since I was child
when I tore out pages of a magazine
and scribbled
"I want to die" over and over
with a washable Crayola marker.

I almost killed myself
two weeks ago
and I'm not happy
but happy doesn't always
mean better.

I almost killed myself
two weeks ago
and today I see a life worth living.

Native tongue

"I feel like the color of the walls"
and I no longer care
if that is misunderstood.
This is a phrase in my mother tongue
the one where I am the only
native speaker.

I have spent too long
translating
to be more relatable,
watering myself down
for the web of dialects.

My people will know
"I feel like the color of the walls"
to be precise language
because their languages
have similar roots.

They know that
"I feel like the color of the walls"
does not mean
"I feel like eggshell white."

They will not suppose me random
because they could not see
where I was or
where I was going.
They know there is care

in how I speak
when I am not hurried
to translate.

If they have questions,
they will be patient,
they will trust that the context clues
will reveal themselves in time.

Or they will trust that
what I need more than
direct translations
is to be heard,
to be felt.
That is the only way
my language will survive
my life.

I will learn
to stop translating
for the people who do not
know how to be quiet.

I will overcome
this assimilation.

Hideaway

I long for
what I've never known:
a warm love beside me
as I'm curled up in bed
with the voice of Billie Eilish
floating along the
current of the fan
while the fatigue is still
heavy in my lungs.

They hold me,
but don't rub circles
on my back
because they know in
gentle repetitive contact,
I can't find comfort,
just screaming nerves.
They'll place kisses
on my neck
and press their thumbs
into the knots
they'll know
linger under the skin
because the weight of
holding up my own skull
is the workout that
the doctors don't care about.
When I try to talk,
they'll remind me gently

that I don't have to fill
the silence. I should rest.
when I wake up
we don't have to rush
out of bed.
We can stay there a little longer.
They won't rush away from
accompanying me
in the place
I can't leave.

They make a pact not to fall
asleep until I have
because the loneliness
of this exhaustion
is worse than the weight in my blood.
And if the dogs need to go out,
they'd take care of them,
creeping out with a
kiss on my forehead,
but they wouldn't use it
as an excuse to
not come back.

And if I can't sleep,
if the frustration burns
tears through my eyes,
they'll pull me into their lap
and read me stories from

Cosmicomics.
They'll power through
the impossible names
because I love hearing
how people find ways to
pronounce them.
And they'll tell me how much
they love spending this
time with me.

And when my hips
start to hurt,
their eyes would spark
and we'd turn me onto my stomach
so they can get their hands
on my butt to rub it.
Maybe they'd give it a jiggle
and we'd laugh.
And maybe the rub wouldn't help,
but at least my pain
wouldn't be useless.

I don't think it's too much
to long for a love to hideaway
with me.

Maybe this bed wouldn't feel
like a tomb
if it was a relation-ship.

Perfect partner

I don't think
that my standards
are too high

All I want
is someone with
lots of patience
and the ability to
communicate
when that patience
is running thin
and what they need
for it to not
disappear
entirely.

I want someone
that can remind me
that there's still
laughter to be had
even when my life
feels devoid of joy.

They'll still make moves
on me even if I've
been in a rut for
a month
or two
because I'm still

worth desiring.

I'll never have to
question
how they feel about me
or if all our plans
will fall apart
in the lap
of someone else.

When I dream big
they will dare me
to dream bigger
and will help me
sort the pieces
I already know
that I have
or know how
to get.

They'll do their
homework
without me
having to ask.
They'll read
everything they can
on my diagnoses
but they'll never
play expert.

They'll learn
so that when I'm
a puddle on the carpet
they'll know
how to help me
clean myself up.
and they'll learn
and learn
and learn
until it becomes
second nature.

And more than anything
I want my perfect partner
to be me.

Love is not without burden

Love is not free from burden.
The people who know that,
we carry each other's weights
as best we can
using the threads that bind us.
Eventually, these threads become
the net that catches and cradles
instead of the single thread
to balance and break.

At the end of it all,
all our burdens
will be buried in the ground
with what was the remains
of everyone and everything.
Our burdens will mean nothing.
You look out into the sky,
into this infinity
that we're bathed in
and it too unweaves the meaning
out of our burdens.
It takes the meaning
from everything.
If there's no meaning,
there is only
what is.

And what is
are these arms

held open for your grief,
their home
with the spare bedroom
made up in case
anyone can't go home,
his jokes
filling a belly
with laughter boiling the rage
to soften it,
her gaze
held tight and soft
in the face
of your shame,
and this community
full of weirdos and rejects
who won't turn away from
who you are and
the burdens you bring.

What is is not fate
or destiny
or divinity.
What is is nature
and a woven series of choices.
And I choose
to be here with you
and you
and you
and your burdens

and love you.

There's no divine salvation,
but there's a place for you here now.
You don't have to earn it.
If there is no meaning,
then there is no point to hiding.
Let us know you and your burdens
and we will love you
all the more for it.
Love does not come without burdens,
love is what helps you carry them.

Whole body

I no longer care
if I gain weight.
You tell me that
I have no self-control
and I say good!
That is what has kept me
from withering away!
This thing you call wrong
has saved my life!
I am not broken!
Your perception of me is!
And I will not play
to your distortions!
I am whole!
And I am mighty!
And I am thick with triumph!

You can sculpt yourself down
to your perfect aesthetic,
always anxious of the eyes on you,
but these legs will carry me
over mountains,
these arms will give
the best hugs,
this fat will keep me warm
when depression chills me.

Who am I to tell nature
that it is wrong

if it no longer wants me
to have a small body?
I am no longer a child
whose ribs show
from the upward stretch
of adolescence.
I will no longer measure
my self-worth
by whether or not
I am fuckable
for no longer looking
like my child self.
I will not live in fear
of becoming too big
for you to touch.

Be grateful that this body
has plentiful places
to hold
because the alternative
may leave you grabbing
at dirt instead.

Self-love

This is an act of self-love,
standing here, shaking,
rediscovering why
I am so goddamn cool.

How fucking sick
it is that I can bleed up here
and people throw snaps.
This is a public leeching.

I've spent five years
trying to forget and
remember myself
but I've been here.

There's been no need
to break myself down
into bite-sized pieces
because those pieces are jagged.
You're better off choking.

I've spent five,
maybe ten,
maybe twenty years
learning to play human
instead of owning
that I am a god.

What else could contain
inside itself
this much loathing
and still show love?

Who else could be in the
driver's seat
whizzing by telephone poles
with hungry eyes,
and still vow to
feast upon Hell
to spit out
something greater?

The god of motherfucking cool.

When the doctors ask
do you experience racing thoughts,
I tell them no, I've already won.

I don't need *your* hobbies,
your sports,
your playlists
to make me interesting.
I am interesting on *my* own.
I've got the power
of good conversation
locked down.
I could spend an eon

in my pajamas
on the couch
but you pick my brain apart
and I would still be
fucking fascinating.

To anyone who thinks
that I am weak
for thinking thoughts of dying,
I am a god of many strengths:
I'm fortified by my fighting.

So, give your offering
as retribution
for this leeching
and for this breaking
because my divinity
cannot be contained
no matter how much I try.
Self-love
and divinity
cannot fill my stomach.
So, your coin will do,
but applause works too.

I want to make them laugh

I want to make them laugh
again and again
until their cheeks hurt
and their eyes are bright blue
from tears—
a laugh that would normally
leave them saying
"I haven't laughed like that
in so long."
But they wouldn't be able to say that,
because I made them laugh
yesterday
and last week
and every other Saturday,
and I'm going to keep at it
because their smile,
oh, their smile
it could light up
every corn town
like the one they came from.

It could light the book lights
for all the dreamers
traveling away from
their pain,
the desk lamps
where they scribble out
their own worlds
and their stories

and their sorrows—
the stories where their pain
means something
other than just to hurt.
A story where the pain
has an end
because they can't imagine one
for themselves;
a story for every kid
that was just like them.
They know that the ecstasy
of fellowship has its costs,
tiny hand in tiny hand
until they grow apart.

And yet they still laugh.
They still look in the mirror
and say,
"Thank you for finding the joy."
And I say back,
"Thank you for giving it meaning."

www.ingramcontent.com/pod-product-compliance
Lightning Source LLC
Chambersburg PA
CBHW070223180726
47999CB00017B/1957